3D ORIGAMI FUN!

Stephanie Martyn

Adamsmedia

AVON, MASSACHUSETTS

Published by
Adams Media, a division of F+W Media, Inc.
57 Littlefield Street, Avon, MA 02322. U.S.A.
www.adamsmedia.com

ISBN 10: 1-4405-9031-1
ISBN 13: 978-1-4405-9031-3
eISBN 10: 1-4405-9032-X
eISBN 13: 978-1-4405-9032-0

Printed in the United States of America.

10   9   8   7   6   5   4   3   2

Library of Congress Cataloging-in-Publication Data

Martyn, Stephanie.
    3D origami fun! / Stephanie Martyn.
        pages cm
    Includes index.
    ISBN 978-1-4405-9031-3 (pb) -- ISBN 1-4405-9031-1 (pb) -- ISBN 978-1-4405-9032-0 (ebook) -- ISBN
978-1-4405-9032-X (ebook)
    1. Origami. I. Title.
    TT872.5.M355 2015
    736'.982--dc23
                        2015015391

Many of the designations used by manufacturers and sellers to distinguish their products are claimed as trademarks. Where those designations appear in this book and F+W Media, Inc. was aware of a trademark claim, the designations have been printed with initial capital letters.

Cover design by Frank Rivera.
Cover photos by Elisabeth Lariviere.
Interior photos by Stephanie Martyn and Elisabeth Lariviere.

This book is available at quantity discounts for bulk purchases.
For information, please call 1-800-289-0963.

Dedication

For Leah, Jackie, Jaeson, and Aria

Acknowledgment

Thank you, Marsha Ziegler, for "pockets."

Contents

Introduction

Three-dimensional origami is a unique paper-folding art. Unlike typical origami folding, where a single sheet of paper is folded into a particular shape, 3D origami is made up of hundreds—sometimes even thousands—of individually folded pieces. These folded pieces are joined together to create a final masterpiece that is extremely sturdy—and fun!

3D origami does take time and patience, but the results are well worth the effort. You may actually find the cutting and folding process relaxing! You can even multitask, and cut or fold the paper while you're listening to music or an audiobook. The building process itself is simple, and you'll find it easy to follow with the photos and diagrams in this book.

This type of origami is perfect for people of all ages, and it's a great activity idea for parties or get-togethers. Choose a project that fits in with the theme of your party, and you've got a memorable activity and a party favor all in one. Hosting a beach-themed party in the summer? Invite guests to make seashells. Celebrate with cupcakes at an older child's birthday party. Baby shower guests will love creating cute little chicks to celebrate the little one on the way! (If you're hosting a party, consider cutting and/or folding the basic paper pieces ahead of time so guests can jump right into the building process.)

Since they're handmade, 3D origami projects also make great gifts. Have a child make an apple for his teacher. Bring a colorful butterfly to a neighbor. Construct a silly monkey for a friend who needs a laugh. Surprise a wise coworker by leaving an owl on her desk. Each present is sure to bring a smile to the recipient's face.

In this book, you will learn how to cut the paper, fold it into basic 3D origami pieces, and then glue the pieces together to form an adorable homemade piece of art. Each project is customizable—the photos here give you a guideline, but feel free to use your own color choices, and add small details to the finished product to really make it your own. For even more ideas, visit Stinkin' Kute Origami on Facebook (*www.facebook.com/stinkinkuteorigami*). Let's get cutting and folding!

Chapter 1
THE BASICS OF 3D ORIGAMI

Types of Paper

The great thing about 3D origami is you can use many different types of paper for folding. However, the thickness and size of the paper will affect the outcome of your structure. Paper is sold by weight, which measures the thickness and strength of the paper. For the most part, the higher the number, the thicker and stronger the paper.

Most of the projects in this book use 24-pound paper, which can be purchased online or in office stores. You could use regular 20-pound printer paper for most projects, but it might deliver less sturdy results. Construction paper (typically 65–80 pounds) is not recommended for most 3D origami, as it tears easily and can be difficult to fold crisply. Scrapbooking paper is considered "heavyweight" and usually is around 80 pounds; therefore, it's not appropriate for 3D origami.

For each project in this book, you'll find the thickness of paper that I recommend within the materials list. Use cardstock (65–80 pounds) for glued-on facial features and limbs.

Buying Paper

You can purchase paper for these projects online or in office stores. I suggest buying an assorted pack that comes with a variety of colors. I have good experience using Xerox Multipurpose Color Paper and Astrobrights. You'll find them in reams of 500 sheets and the cost ranges from $9–$16. Black and brown 24-pound paper is difficult to find in stores, but you can purchase it on Amazon.com. You may substitute patterned paper as long as the weight is appropriate. Keep in mind that patterned paper might affect how your art is distinguished, so plan your colors before you start.

Cutting Tools

Although you can use scissors to cut the paper, a paper trimmer will deliver quicker and more accurate results. You will, however, need scissors for some of the smaller, finer cuts. If you're going to use scissors, be sure your pair is sharp and fits your hand properly.

You can find many styles of paper trimmers at local craft stores. Your best bet is a 12" Personal Paper Trimmer from Carl, which costs less than $20. Any similar model will work and is safe for kids to use since the blade is concealed. Most models come with an extra blade, too.

I wouldn't advise spending too much on a nice paper trimmer simply because frayed edges won't show in a 3D origami structure. I have been using the same paper trimmer for more than five years, so even the inexpensive ones last awhile!

Organizing Your Paper

If you plan to make several 3D origami structures, it's a good idea to organize your paper, whether it's simply cut or already folded. Once I decide what project I'm going to tackle, the first thing I do is cut my paper. To keep things neat, I store my cut paper in a zip-top bag. As I begin folding, I keep my folded pieces in a neat pile on the table, or I put them back into the same zip-top bag if I'm not going to construct at that moment. I keep different colors in different bags. Even though there is a noticeable difference in size between A and B paper, consider labeling the size on the bag so you can easily find what you need.

If you are the type who likes to plan ahead for future projects, you might consider buying nifty plastic storage containers that will hold a good amount of your cut and folded paper. I use the Darice Adjustable Storage Box, which you can find at local craft stores—it only costs about $10. I especially like the ones with adjustable dividers.

How to Cut Size A Paper

This technique of cutting paper is efficient because it uses a complete 8.5" × 11" sheet of paper with no waste. One sheet of paper yields 24 pieces of Size A folding paper. These instructions demonstrate how to cut 1 piece of paper, but keep in mind that you can cut multiple sheets at once to increase the amount of pieces you make. The number of pieces of paper you can stack is dependent upon the thickness of the paper. I can usually cut 5 sheets of 24-pound paper and 8 sheets of 20-pound paper with my paper trimmer.

Materials

* Paper Cutter (or scissors)
* 1 (8.5" × 11") Sheet

....

1. Start by cutting your 8.5" × 11" sheet of paper in half to make 2 (4.25" × 5.5") rectangles.

2. Stack the 2 pieces of paper from the previous step and cut them in half the short way.

3. Stack the 4 pieces of paper from the previous step and cut in half the long way.

4. You now have 8 pieces of paper. Take 1 piece and fold it accordion style, making sure that it's even (the creased lines will serve as a cutting mark).

5. Stack the creased paper on top of the remaining unfolded pieces and cut along the creased lines.

6. Repeat this step until you have all pieces cut into thirds.

7. You now have 24 pieces of Size A, $2\frac{11}{16}$" × $1\frac{3}{8}$" (6.5 × 3.5 cm), paper!

How to Cut Size B Paper

This technique is similar to that of cutting Size A paper—again, it's very efficient, with no wasted paper. The difference is that the final dimensions of Size B paper are much smaller, so there are a few more steps. One sheet of 8.5" × 11" paper yields 48 pieces, twice as many as Size A. Since the size of the paper gets pretty small in the last steps, you might find that scissors are easier to use than a paper cutter. These instructions demonstrate how to cut 1 piece of paper, but multiple sheets of paper can be cut at a time to multiply the amount of pieces you create.

Materials

* Paper Cutter
* 1 (8.5" × 11") Sheet
* Scissors

1. Start by using the paper cutter to cut the 8.5" × 11" sheet of paper in half the short way to make 2 (4.25" × 5.5") rectangles.

2. Stack the 2 pieces of paper from the previous step and cut in half the short way, using the paper cutter.

continued on next page

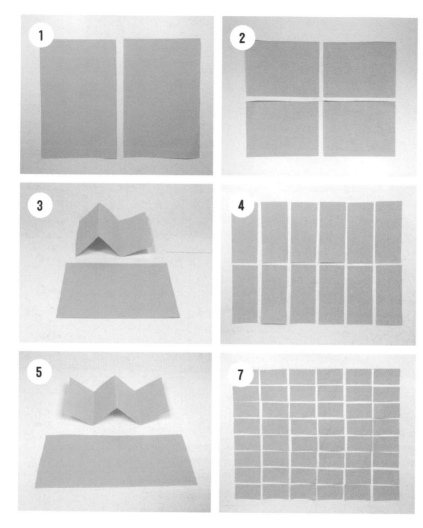

3. You have 4 pieces of paper. Take 1 of the pieces and fold it the short way, accordion style, making sure that it's even. These creases will serve as a cutting mark. Unfold the piece and stack it on top of the 3 unfolded pieces. Cut along the creased lines using the paper cutter. This will make a total of 12 pieces.

4. You should have 12 slim pieces of paper.

5. Now, you're going to cut each piece equally into 4 pieces. Start by taking a piece and folding it in half the long way. Take one end of the paper and fold it back toward the inner fold. Flip and do the same with the opposite side. You are folding it accordion style (evenly) and will be using the creases as guidelines for cutting.

6. Unfold the piece and stack it on top of some unfolded pieces (the amount of pieces you cut at a time is dependent on the thickness of the paper; 2–4 is usually enough). Cut along the lines with scissors. If you find it difficult to cut with scissors, decrease the amount of papers you have stacked.

7. You now have 48 pieces of Size B, $1\frac{15}{16}$" × $1\frac{1}{16}$", paper!

How to Fold a 3D Origami Piece

Even though the size of your folding paper may change, the folding technique remains the same. Size A paper is used in this demonstration. Your goal is to end up with a neatly folded triangle-shaped piece with 2 pockets.

Materials

* 3D Origami Folding Paper

1. Take a piece of Size A paper and fold it in half the long way.

2. From here on out, it's important that the opening to this folded piece is facing down. Fold down the middle the short way to make a crease, then unfold.

3. Fold down half the piece at an angle (on both sides of the crease) so that the folded edge lines up to the crease in the middle. Be sure not to overlap these folds.

4. Flip the piece over.

5. Fold the bottom right corner up diagonally.

6. Repeat symmetrically on the other side. Be sure not to overlap onto the top half, otherwise the pockets won't turn out properly.

continued on next page

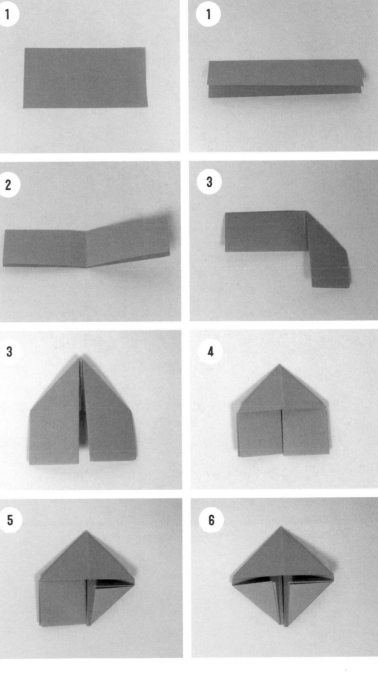

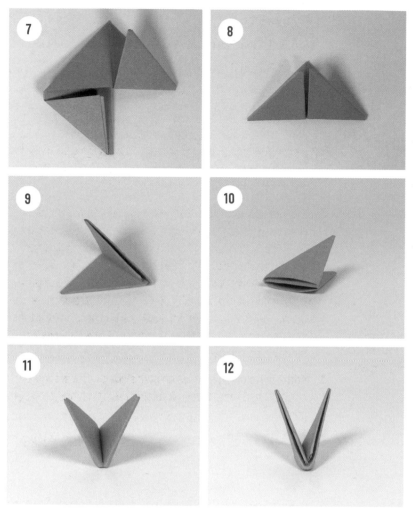

7. Fold one bottom triangle upward.

8. Fold the other bottom triangle upward so the whole piece now looks like a triangle.

9. Fold across the middle. (Flaps should be on the inside of the triangle.) Ta-da! Your 3D origami piece is complete.

10. These are the "pockets" for constructing. This is where the "points" will be inserted.

11. This is the "smooth side" of a 3D origami piece. It's shown by a **Λ** in the diagrams for each project.

12. This is the "rough side" of a 3D origami piece. It's shown by a **V** in the diagrams for each project.

How to Construct a Base

The secret to a sturdy 3D origami structure is having a solid base. It may take some time getting used to manipulating the small folded pieces to fit into each other's pockets and points, but with practice and persistence, this process will become second nature. It is important to glue your base as you construct it. 3D origami structures start off fragile in the beginning, but you will notice that as you continue building, the structure becomes amazingly sturdy. The number of pieces that goes into a base depends on the specific design. This one uses 20 pieces in each row. Technically, only the orange pieces make up the base, but it's necessary to have the blue pieces (row 1) to hold the base together. To keep things simple, we'll consider row 1 as part of the base. Thus, 2 rows of paper make up the base. Refer to the diagram or instructions for each specific project for further information.

Materials

* Size A Folded Pieces (for foundation of base)
* Size A Folded Pieces (for row 1)
* All-Purpose Glue

....

1. Hold 2 folded Size A origami pieces next to each other with their points facing up and smooth sides facing you. These orange pieces represent the foundation of the base. These pieces will not be visible in most structures.

2. You will now add a piece to row 1 of your structure. This is represented by the blue piece. Use your finger to wedge open the bottom pockets of the blue piece. This will make it much easier to insert the orange points. Now place a dab of glue between the points of the orange piece, where your orange and blue pieces will connect. Face the blue piece in the opposite direction (rough side toward you) and insert the orange points into the blue pockets. Push the blue piece as far down as you can.

3. Add 2 more orange pieces on both sides of your working circle. Glue 2 more blue pieces onto the points of the orange piece.

continued on next page

4. Continue repeating step 3. Don't forget to add glue during these crucial steps; it will keep your base from slipping apart.

5. Once you reach the amount of pieces you need in a row for your base (orange), join both sides with a final piece (blue) to connect the circle.

6. Row 2 should have the same amount of pieces as your base and row 1 (unless your design tells you to increase/decrease).

7. The base will start to shape itself as you work your way up and add more rows. You can help it along by shaping it so that you create a flat bottom (orange pieces). This can be done by scrunching the blue pieces together so their points are facing down. As you do this, you'll see the pockets of the orange pieces rise in the middle. The pocket edge of the orange pieces make up the flat bottom.

8. Now flip it over so the orange part is on the bottom and the blue pieces are pointing upward. Your base is complete! Build upward from this while following your project's colored diagram and see a work of art form before your eyes. Photos show two different angles.

Getting Started

Not all the projects will have a base. For each project that does, refer to its diagram for the number of pieces you will need in each row and what colors to use in row 1. Then follow the "How to Construct a Base" instructions.

All the projects in the book are easily mastered in no time! But here's a rough guideline of which might be good designs to start with as you build up to more complicated projects.

Simple Beginner Projects

- Bumblebee
- Seashell
- Crab
- Spider
- Watermelon
- Strawberry
- Owl

Intermediate Designs

- Apple
- Pig
- Baby Chick
- Panda
- Cupcake
- Tiger
- Caterpillar
- Ladybug
- Butterfly
- Sea Turtle
- Elephant
- Sunflower

For Experienced Builders

- Clownfish
- Octopus
- Pineapple
- Monkey
- Giraffe
- Cow

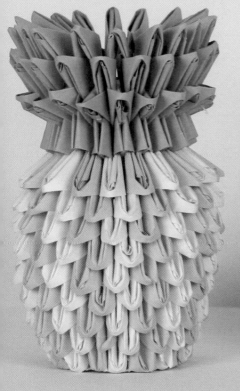

Strawberry

If you're just starting to learn 3D origami, the Strawberry is a great first project to tackle. The pattern is simple but the results are very impressive. If you follow this pattern with the correct paper size and weight, the Strawberry will end up 2" wide and 2.5" tall.

Materials

* 70 Size A Red Folded Pieces (24 lb. paper)

* 10 Size A Green Folded Pieces (24 lb. paper)

* 9 (3 × 1.5 cm) Black Folded Pieces (24 lb. paper)—these pieces will be folded the same way as the Size A and B pieces

* All-Purpose Glue

Pattern Key
V Rough side facing out
✱ Where your 3 × 1.5 cm folded pieces will be inserted (seeds)

1. In order to achieve a better "strawberry" shape, this pattern doesn't start with the basic 3D origami base. Instead, start the base with all the pieces facing the same direction (rough side facing out).

2. As you build, the piece on top will connect and join 2 pieces from the bottom.

3. Once you've reached 10 pieces across row 1, join both sides with the final piece from row 2.

4. Use the diagram to continue constructing from the bottom up. Remember to glue each piece as you construct. Each row will have 10 pieces. For now, ignore the * in the diagram. This represents the seeds (black pieces) that will be added after the structure is complete.

5. The top final row will be green and comes to a tight close on its own.

6. Now that the body and stem of your Strawberry are complete, it's time to add the seeds. Use a ruler to measure the 3 × 1.5 cm black rectangles. Cut carefully with scissors. To conserve time, you can first cut out 1 rectangle and use that as a cutting guideline for the additional 8 pieces. Use the same folding instructions from Chapter 1 to fold these pieces.

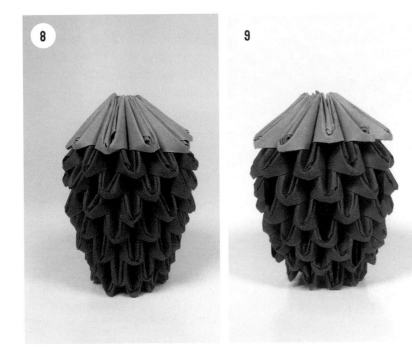

7. Take your black 3 × 1.5 cm folded pieces and tuck them one by one into their designated holes, following the * in the diagram.

8. Glue into place.

9. Done! It looks almost as good as the real thing.

WATERMELON

Watermelon

Watermelon is a perennial favorite summertime fruit. This paper version is even better than the original—it's neater and the seeds are no trouble at all. This is one of my favorite 3D origami projects and makes a great artsy gift for any age. Be sure to carefully glue the pieces as you construct. This will prevent the structure from being too loose and falling apart, especially since it's not built upward like most other projects. As described, your slice will be about 5" wide and 6" tall when finished.

Materials

* 109 Size A Dark Pink Folded Pieces (24 lb. paper)

* 16 Size A White Folded Pieces (24 lb. paper)

* 52 Size A Green Folded Pieces (24 lb. paper)

* 9 Size A Black Folded Pieces (24 lb. paper)

* All-Purpose Glue

Key
Λ Smooth side facing out (these pieces will be part of the Watermelon's rind)
V Rough side facing out

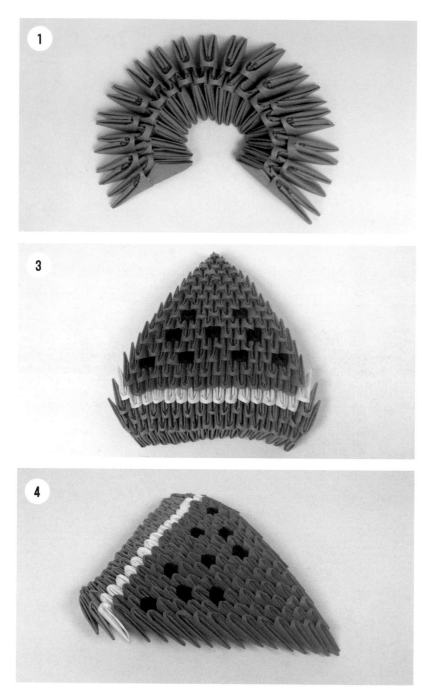

1. The Watermelon will be constructed from the rind to the flesh. Follow the directions for "How to Construct a Base" in Chapter 1, but instead of joining both sides and making a circle, leave them unconnected. Use 17 pieces where Chapter 1 shows orange pieces, and use 16 pieces for the row 1 (shown in blue in Chapter 1). Since there is a decrease in pieces between the base and row 1, you will have an extra point at both ends. With the increase in pieces in row 2, the extra outer pockets will be inserted into the extra points. Although it will curl at first, it will straighten up as you continue constructing.

2. Follow the color pattern in the diagram and construct upward from the rind. Each folded piece added to a new row should conjoin 2 pieces from the previous. Don't forget to glue!

3. As you move your way up, each new row will have 1 less piece than the last.

4. What you will end up with is a row with 1 piece—the tip of the Watermelon!

APPLE

Apple

This piece makes a perfect gift for your favorite teacher. This structure uses thick cardstock paper instead of the usual 24-pound paper. Cardstock is more difficult to fold compared to 24-pound paper, but because of its thickness, fewer pieces are required overall. Cardstock is ideal for this design because of the bulky and solid look it delivers—the Apple will hold up for years on a teacher's desk. It ends up about 2.5" wide and 3" tall.

Materials

* 88 Size A Red Folded Pieces (65 lb. cardstock)
* 2 Size A Green Folded Pieces (24 lb. paper)
* All-Purpose Glue
* 1 (3.5" × 8") Brown Unfolded Piece (24 lb. paper)
* Transparent Adhesive Tape

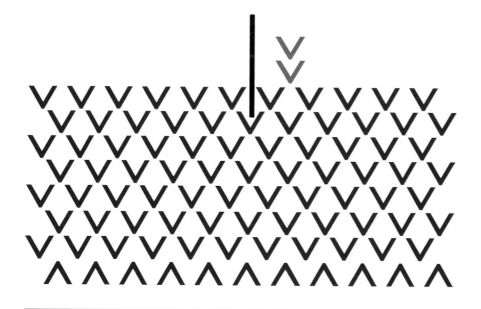

Key
∧ Smooth side facing out (these pieces will not be visible when the structure is complete since they serve as a foundation for the structure to be built on)
∨ Rough side facing out

1. Start this Apple by building a basic 3D origami base. (See the instructions for "How to Construct a Base" in Chapter 1.) Use 11 red pieces where Chapter 1 shows orange pieces, and use 11 red pieces for row 1 (shown in blue in Chapter 1).

2. Once the base is complete, build upward until you have 7 completed rows of red pieces. There will be 11 pieces in each row. Glue as you go. Each folded piece added to a new row should join 2 pieces from the previous. This image shows the Apple after you've finished the 7 rows.

3. Join and glue the 2 green pieces. This will be the leaf.

4. With the smooth sides facing outward, insert the leaf into the top of the Apple. Use glue to secure the piece in place.

5. Take the brown piece of paper and roll it up tightly the long way. This will be the stem. Use a piece of tape to secure the bottom of the stem (which will not be visible). Insert the stem all the way down into the top opening of the Apple.

6. Your 3D origami Apple is complete!

PINEAPPLE

Pineapple

The rough, ridged surface of 3D origami complements this fruit perfectly. This piece is a bit more challenging to construct because of the different techniques utilized in the Pineapple's green stalk. Gluing your pieces as you construct will hold everything together. Using two different shades of yellow really gives the Pineapple a defined surface with some depth. If you can't find a golden yellow, try a light brown paper instead. This piece works well as decor for a luau or tropical-themed party! At a finished size of 3" wide and 5" tall, this is a unique design element that won't dominate your tables.

Materials

* 90 Size A Yellow Folded Pieces (24 lb. paper)
* 99 Size A Golden Yellow Folded Pieces (24 lb. paper)
* 72 Size A Green Folded Pieces (24 lb. paper)
* All-Purpose Glue

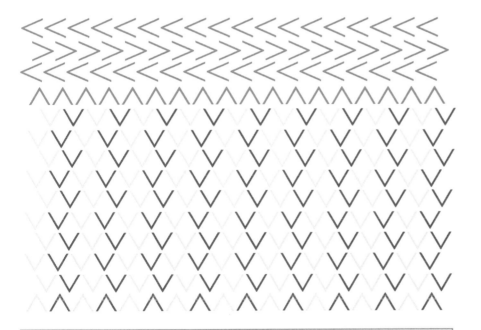

Key
Λ Smooth side facing out (these pieces will not be visible when the structure is complete since they serve as a foundation for the structure to be built on)
V Rough side facing out
< or > Upside down and rough side facing out; pockets should be facing up

1. Start this Pineapple with the basic 3D origami base. (See the instructions on "How to Construct a Base" in Chapter 1.) Use 18 pieces where Chapter 1 shows orange pieces and 18 pieces for row 1 (shown in blue in Chapter 1). There will be a total of 9 rows. See the Pineapple Diagram for color placement. Each piece added should connect and join 2 pieces from the previous. Don't forget to glue!

2. For the stalk (green pieces), start by facing the pieces smooth side out.

3. The pieces will be inserted rough side out and upside down. Build on top of the previous row by inserting the folds of your building pieces into the points of the previous rows. Use glue in each spot.

4. For the next 2 rows, the pieces will be upside down with the points inserted into the openings of the previous row's pieces. Every piece added will connect to 2 different pieces from the previous row. This will give a total of 3 rows using an upside-down insertion technique.

5. Make sure all pieces are secure with glue. Finished!

CUPCAKE

Cupcake

Chocolate or vanilla? You can make this Cupcake whatever flavor you want—and you don't need to worry about calories! This pattern will give you a 2.5" wide and 3" tall chocolate cupcake with pink icing and a cherry on top, but feel free to change the colors around to suit your liking—or that of the person having a birthday. Substitute the brown with yellow or tan to get a vanilla cake. Perhaps change your frosting to a different color and top it off with a blue pompom instead. The possibilities are endless!

Materials

* 54 Size A Brown Folded Pieces (24 lb. paper)
* 99 Size A Pink Folded Pieces (24 lb. paper)
* All-Purpose Glue
* 1 Small Red Pompom

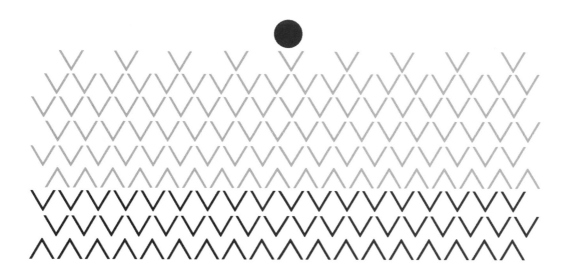

Key

∧ Smooth side facing out (these pieces will not be visible when the structure is complete since they serve as a foundation for the structure to be built on)

∨ Rough side facing out

---

1. Start the Cupcake with a basic 3D origami base. (See the instructions for "How to Construct a Base" in Chapter 1.) There will be 18 brown pieces in the foundation row (shown in orange in Chapter 1) and 18 brown pieces in row 1 (shown in blue in Chapter 1). Complete the cake portion of the cupcake with one more row of brown pieces. Each folded piece added to a new row should join 2 pieces from the previous. Glue as you go.

2. In the next row, pink pieces will be inserted smooth side facing out. This row will not really be visible when your structure is complete because it serves as a foundation to "restart" your base. The purpose is to create a bump in your structure to differentiate the cake from the frosting.

3. For the icing of the Cupcake, there will be 4 full rows of pink pieces. When you've reached row 5, insert a pink piece in every other position. This will create a closing at the top of the Cupcake.

4. Use all-purpose glue to attach the red pompom to the top of your Cupcake. The ripples of the paper are very reminiscent of interesting frosting patterns.

Chapter 3
ZOO ANIMALS

PANDA

Panda

Who doesn't love an adorable panda bear? You'll use more than 500 pieces for this design, but the final 6.5" tall product is really awe-inspiring, especially with the pop of color from the Panda's bamboo accessory. I recommend using 24-pound paper for both the white and black pieces. Substituting other thicknesses of paper will alter the results of the final structure. For example, substituting white 20-pound standard printing paper might cause the structure to be slightly lopsided since it will build differently than the 24-pound black pieces. Because of its thickness, use 65-pound cardstock for the ears, arms, and eyes.

Materials

* 410 Size A White Folded Pieces (24 lb. paper)

* 136 Size A Black Folded Pieces (24 lb. paper)

* All-Purpose Glue

* 13 Size A Green Folded Pieces (24 lb. paper)

* Scissors

* White and Black Paper (65 lb. cardstock)—for eyes

* Hot Glue Gun

* 1 Black Pompom (nose)

* Black Paper (65 lb. cardstock)— for arms and ears

Key
Λ Smooth side facing out (These pieces will not be visible when the structure is complete since they serve as a foundation for the structure to be built on)
V Rough side facing out
I Placement of arms
* Placement of nose
Black Circles Placement of ears

1. Start this Panda with the basic 3D origami base. (See the instructions for "How to Construct a Base" in Chapter 1.) Use 17 pieces where Chapter 1 shows orange pieces, and use 26 pieces for row 1 (shown in blue in Chapter 1). The bottom row (foundation row) in the diagram will not be visible when the structure is complete, so the color does not matter. Don't forget to glue as you go.

2. Build upward from the foundation. You will have 8 rows of white pieces, followed by 3 rows of black pieces. This completes the body of the Panda.

3. Construct a row with the pieces facing smooth side out. Be sure to glue each piece to the structure. The pieces in this row will not be visible once the structure is complete. Facing the pieces this way creates a new foundation on which you'll build the head.

4. Follow the Panda Diagram to build the head. You'll start with white pieces, rough side out.

5. Continue building the rest of the rows to finish the head.

6. Now it's time to make the bamboo stalk. Follow the diagram and glue as you construct.

7 **8** **9**

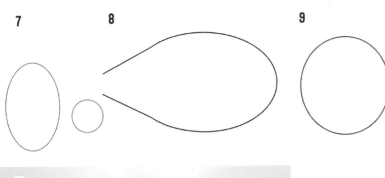

7. Cut out the eye shapes. Use hot glue to attach the eyes and pompom (nose) to the structure.

8. Cut out and use all-purpose glue to attach the arms to the structure (see the diagram for placement).

9. Cut out and attach the Panda's ears with all-purpose glue.

10. Use hot glue to attach the bamboo to the front of one of the Panda's paws.

MONKEY

Monkey

This silly 4.5" tall Monkey has the cutest little face and ears. Monkeys are always popular animals with kids, so this project is a great addition to a jungle-themed party or bedroom decor. It's difficult to find brown paper in stores, but don't substitute construction paper. You'll probably have to buy the 24-pound brown paper and 20-pound tan paper online instead.

Materials

* 74 Size A Tan Folded Pieces (20 lb. paper)
* 266 Size A Brown Folded Pieces (24 lb. paper)
* All-Purpose Glue
* Scissors
* Brown and White Paper (65 lb. cardstock)—for eyes
* Black Marker
* Brown and Tan Paper (65 lb. cardstock)—for ears
* Brown and Pink Paper (65 lb. cardstock)—for mouth and tongue
* Hot Glue Gun (for facial features)
* Brown Paper (65 lb. cardstock)—for arms and tail

Key

∧ Smooth side facing out (these pieces will not be visible when the structure is complete since they serve as a foundation for the structure to be built on)

V Rough side facing out

＊ Placement of eyes

— Placement of mouth

> and < Placement ears and arms

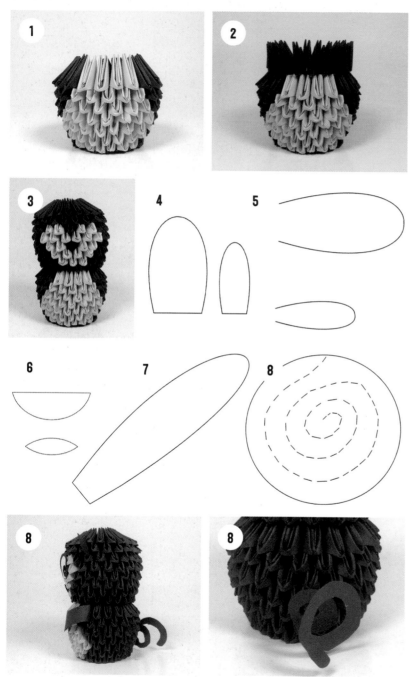

1. Start the base of the Monkey, following the instructions for "How to Construct a Base" in Chapter 1. Use 20 pieces where Chapter 1 shows orange pieces and also 20 pieces for row 1 (shown in blue in Chapter 1). Every row from the bottom up will also have 20 pieces. Each constructing piece will connect 2 pieces from the previous row. Glue as you go.

2. After completing the belly, construct a row with the pieces facing smooth side out. This will serve as a foundation for a new base that will hold the Monkey's head.

3. Continue constructing the head, following the color pattern on the diagram.

4. Cut out the 2 oval shapes for the eyes (the larger in brown paper; the smaller in white). Glue the white paper onto the brown and use a black marker to color the insides of the eyes.

5. Construct the ears with scissors and glue, using brown and tan paper.

6. Use brown paper for the mouth and pink for the tongue. Glue the facial features to the Monkey.

7. Cut out the Monkey's arms and attach with glue.

8. For the tail, cut a circle out of brown paper. Starting from the outside, cut into the circle and make a spiral shape. Glue and insert the inner end of the spiral into the back of the Monkey.

9. This Monkey is ready for some mischief!

ELEPHANT

Elephant

With floppy ears and a peanut in its trunk, this whimsical Elephant is as sturdy as his real-life counterpart. The entire structure of the 4.5" tall Elephant uses gray 20-pound paper. His trunk and facial features give him a quirky, fun personality. I didn't add limbs because I liked the focus on his trunk, but add some to yours if you prefer.

Materials

* 349 Size A Gray Folded Pieces (20 lb. paper)
* All-Purpose Glue
* Hot Glue Gun
* Scissors
* Gray and Pink Paper (65 lb. cardstock)—for ears
* White and Black Paper (65 lb. cardstock)—for eyes
* Black Marker (optional)
* Black and Pink Paper (65 lb. cardstock)—for mouth and tongue
* Tan Paper (65 lb. cardstock)—for peanut

Key
∧ Smooth side facing out (these pieces will not be visible when the structure is complete since they serve as a foundation for the structure to be built on)
∨ Rough side facing out
* Placement of eyes and trunk
— Placement of mouth
| Placement of ears

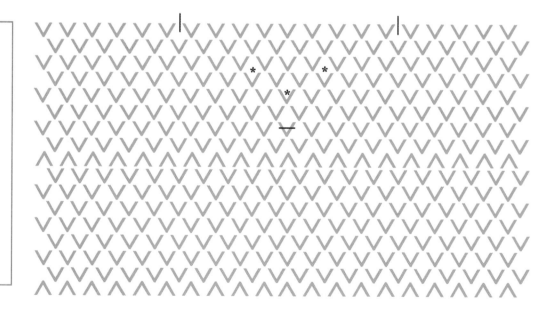

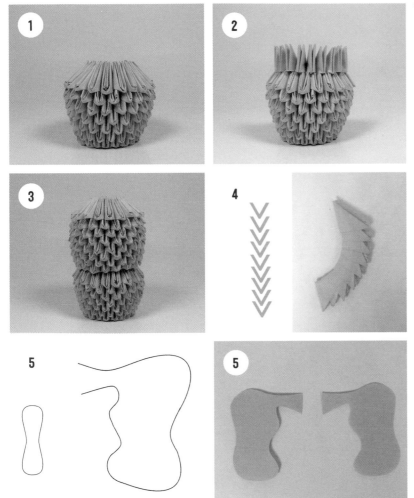

1. Start with your basic 3D origami base using 20 pieces. There will be 20 pieces where Chapter 1 shows orange pieces, and also 20 pieces in row 1 (shown in blue in Chapter 1). (See the instructions for "How to Construct a Base" in Chapter 1.) The bottom row (foundation row) in the diagram will not be visible when the structure is complete. There will be 20 pieces in each row of this Elephant. Each added piece should connect 2 pieces from the previous row.

2. Once you've reached 7 rows (not including the foundation row), construct a row with your pieces facing smooth side out. This will serve as a foundation for the Elephant's head. Glue as you go.

3. Construct 8 more rows to complete the head of the Elephant.

4. Now it's time to build the trunk. To do this, you'll connect and glue 9 gray folded pieces. Form a curve with the pieces as you connect them. Attach the trunk to the Elephant's head using hot glue.

5. Use a pencil to outline the Elephant's ears. Cut with scissors and attach to the Elephant as shown in the diagram.

6   **7**   **8**

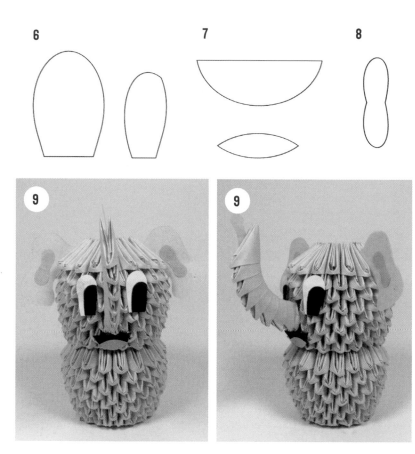

6. Cut out the shape of the Elephant's eyes using white paper. Use black paper for the insides of the eyes (or color in with a black marker).

7. Now, on to his mouth. Use black and pink paper for the mouth and tongue. Use hot glue to attach all the facial features to the structure.

8. Cut a peanut shape out of the tan paper. Use all-purpose glue to attach the "peanut" on the tip of the trunk, in between the points of the outermost piece.

9. All done!

GIRAFFE

Giraffe

Any giraffe design needs to showcase the animal's amazing height! To accomplish that with 3D origami, this 6.5" tall Giraffe uses the basic 3D origami base, but we'll insert the Giraffe's feet under the base. As you build the neck, you will increase 1 row, decrease the next, and repeat this pattern. This is so the neck of the Giraffe remains the same thickness from bottom to top, making it strong.

Materials

* 120 Size A Golden Yellow Folded Pieces (24 lb. paper)
* 89 Size A Brown Folded Pieces (24 lb. paper)
* All-Purpose Glue
* Hot Glue Gun
* Scissors
* Black Paper (65 lb. cardstock)— for eyes

Key

Λ Smooth side facing out (these pieces will not be visible when the structure is complete since they serve as a foundation for the structure to be built on)

V Rough side facing out

∗ Placement of eyes

| Placement of mouth

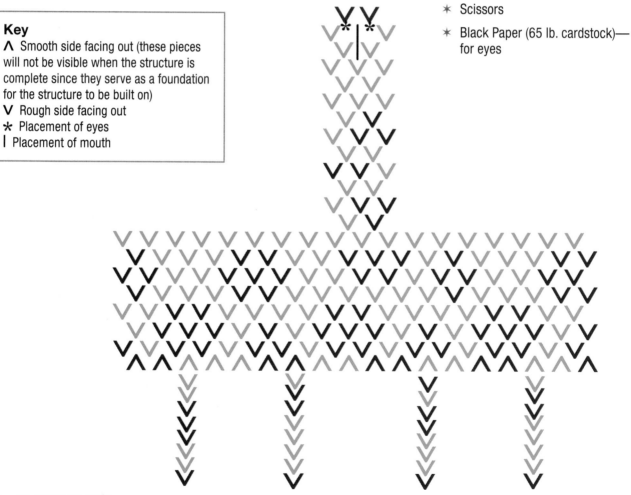

1. Follow the instructions for "How to Construct a Base" in Chapter 1. The orange pieces in Chapter 1 will be substituted with the bottom row in the Giraffe Diagram (there will be 18 pieces). Follow the color pattern in the diagram as you build. Row 2 in the diagram (start of **V** pieces) is shown in Chapter 1 as the blue pieces. Glue as you go.

2. After you've completed the body portion of the Giraffe, it's time to build the neck. Refer to the diagram for specific color patterns. Build the neck upward just like you've done for the body, except in one area (see following). Start with 2 pieces on the first row of the neck, then 3 pieces on the next row. Alternate this pattern back and forth while following the diagram. Remember to glue as you construct! For the rows of 3 pieces, be sure the outer pieces tuck into the points from the previous row of 3.

3. On row 11 of the Giraffe's neck, there will be 2 pieces. Insert each piece so that 3 points fit into its pockets.

4. Insert 2 golden yellow pieces into the outermost points of the previous row. These 2 pieces will be the ears.

5. On the final row, insert two brown pieces so that 4 golden yellow points from the previous 2 rows are inserted into the pockets.

6. Take 2 golden yellow pieces and glue them shut using hot glue.

7. Take these 2 pieces and stack them directly on top of each other. Hot glue the pieces together. This piece will be the mouth of the Giraffe.

8. Use hot glue to attach the Giraffe's mouth where shown on the diagram. The pockets of the pieces will be parallel to the Giraffe, while the "rough" side is facing up and the "smooth" side is facing down.

9. Follow the diagram to build the Giraffe's legs. Insert the points into the pockets of the base pieces, on the bottom side of Giraffe. See the diagram for placement.

10. Cut 2 small circles out of black paper for the Giraffe's eyes. Hot glue the eyes to the structure. See the diagram for placement.

11. This tall creature is ready to roam!

TIGER

Tiger

This adorable feline is trying to be ferocious, but he's just too cute! This structure is simple, but the colors of the belly and stripes require a little more attention to the pattern while constructing. The bright orange in this 3.5" Tiger really makes him stand out in a crowd.

Materials

* 155 Size A Orange Folded Pieces (24 lb. paper)
* 59 Size A Black Folded Pieces (24 lb. paper)
* 85 Size A White Folded Pieces (24 lb. paper)
* All-Purpose Glue
* Scissors
* White and Black Paper (65 lb. cardstock)—for eyes
* 1 Black Pompom (nose)
* Hot Glue Gun
* White and Orange Paper (65 lb. cardstock)—for ears and arms

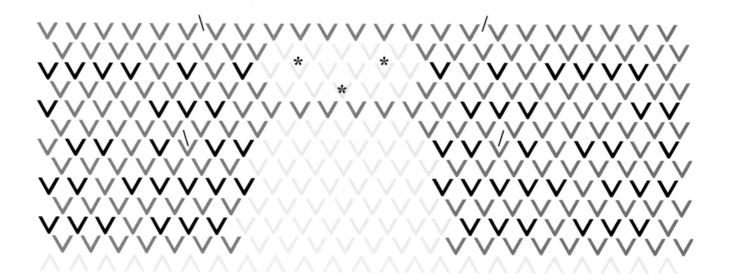

Key
∧ Smooth side facing out (these pieces will not be visible when the structure is complete since they serve as a foundation for the structure to be built on)
∨ Rough side facing out
✳ Placement of eyes and nose
\ and / Placement of ears and arms

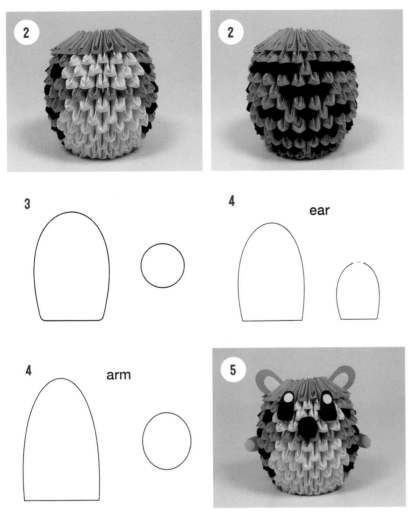

1. Start your basic 3D origami base. Use 23 pieces where Chapter 1 shows orange pieces, and use 23 pieces for row 1 (shown in blue in Chapter 1). The bottom row (foundation row) in the diagram will not be visible when the structure is complete, so the color does not matter. Glue as you go.

2. Continue following the color pattern in the diagram and construct all the way to the top. Once this is complete, you're ready to add the facial features.

3. Use scissors to cut the eyes out of white and black paper. For more accuracy, use a pencil to trace the outline before you cut. Glue the small white circles in the center of the black eye pieces. Use a hot glue gun to glue the eyes and nose (black pompom) to the structure.

4. Cut the ears and arms out of white and orange paper. Hot glue the ears and arms to the structure; see the diagram for placement.

5. Isn't this Tiger so stinkin' cute?!

BUTTERFLY

Butterfly

The 3.5" × 3" Butterfly brings out the essence of 3D origami art. This pattern is unique because it takes 5 separately constructed components and combines them together to make the final structure. The end result is beautiful, and as the artist, you can experiment with different colors to change up the look of the Butterfly. It's important to glue each piece as you construct. The Butterfly lies flat, so it will fall apart easily if not glued.

Materials

* 12 Size B Purple Folded Pieces (24 lb. paper)

* 52 Size B Yellow Folded Pieces (24 lb. paper)

* 60 Size B Blue Folded Pieces (24 lb. paper)

* All-Purpose Glue

* Scissors

* Blue Paper (65 lb. cardstock)—for eyes

* Black Marker

* Hot Glue Gun

* Black Paper (65 lb. cardstock)—for antennae

Key
V Rough side facing upward (structure lies horizontally)
✻ Where the wings and body will attach
Black Sphere Placement of the eyes
Black Lines Placement of the antennae

2

3

4

5

5

5

6

1. The wings of the Butterfly are symmetrical; therefore you will have 2 sets of identical pieces for the left and right halves of this project. It doesn't matter which of the 5 separate parts of the diagram you build first.

2. For all 4 parts of the wings, you will begin with 2 blue folded pieces next to each other and facing the same direction. On the row above, place a yellow piece in the middle slot; it will connect the 2 black pieces. You will "increase" the wing by placing pieces to the left and right of the yellow piece. These pieces will be inserted into the points of the previous row.

3. Continue increasing by attaching pieces to the outer edges of the rows by using the outer "point" from the previous row to connect to.

4. For the larger wings, after you construct the row with 7 pieces, you will need to "decrease" in the next row. You will do this by taking the outer pieces and connecting 3 points, instead of 2. This decrease will also be done for the smaller set of wings after the row with 4 pieces.

5. There will be 11 pieces in the body of the Butterfly. Construct on top of one another as the diagram shows. On the rows where there are 2 pieces, insert the points of the previous piece into the inner folds of the 2 constructing pieces. This will cause the pieces to fan out. These branched-out points will be where the wings connect.

6. The * in the diagram represents where the wings and body will meet. Attach the wings to the body structure with glue.

7

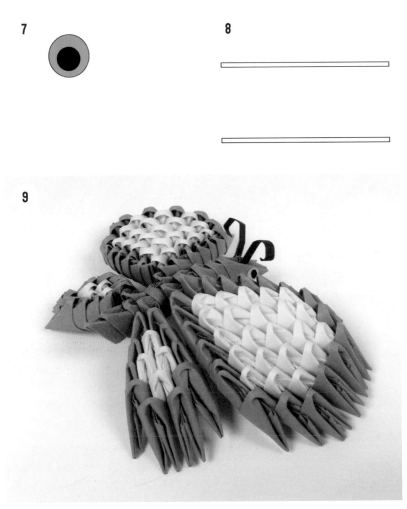

8

9

7. Cut the eyes out of blue paper and fill in the centers with black marker. Use all-purpose glue to attach the eyes onto the end of the body closer to the bigger set of wings.

8. Cut 2 thin strips out of the black paper (approximately 1.5" long). These will be the Butterfly's antennae. Roll the ends of the paper to create a curl at the end. Insert and use all-purpose glue to attach the straight end of the strips into the head of the Butterfly. Be sure the curls are curling out and away from each other.

9. This beautiful creature is ready to fly!

CATERPILLAR

Caterpillar

This cute and crawly 7" Caterpillar is actually 4 different origami structures connected together. This one does require a number of pieces—but it's easy to break up the construction and do one part of the body at a time. Size B pieces are small and can slip apart, so be sure to glue as your construct. Put this little guy alongside the 3D origami Apple, and together they make a cute pair to brighten up a school classroom or child's desk!

Materials

* 448 Size B Green Folded Pieces (24 lb. paper)
* 64 Size B Yellow Folded Pieces (24 lb. paper)
* All-Purpose Glue
* Scissors
* Red Paper (65 lb. cardstock)—for dots (on Caterpillar's back) and nose

* Hot Glue Gun
* 3 Size B Yellow Unfolded Pieces (to connect body parts)
* Black and White Paper (65 lb. cardstock)—for eyes
* Black Paper (65 lb. cardstock)—for mouth
* Black and Purple Paper (65 lb. cardstock)—for antennae

Key

Λ Smooth side facing out (these pieces will not be visible when the structure is complete since they serve as a foundation for the structure to be built on)
V Rough side facing out
✳ Placement of eyes and nose
— Placement of mouth
Black Curved Lines Placement of antennae

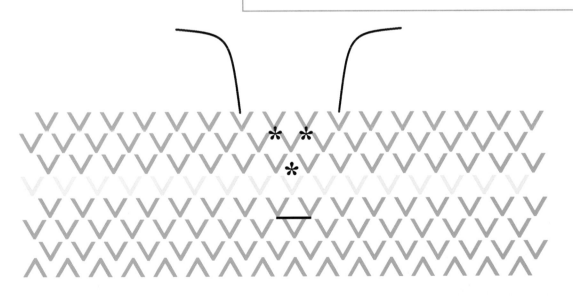

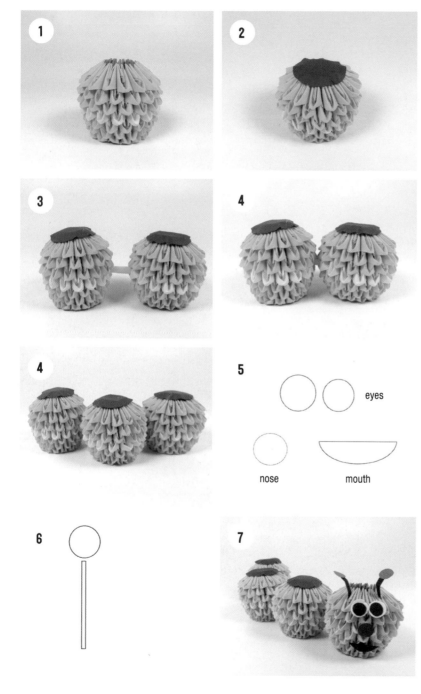

1. Follow the diagram and make 4 of the same patterned structures, starting with a basic base of 16 pieces. There are 16 pieces in every other row too, and each structure has 7 rows. The diagram shows the placement of the facial features, which will only be applied to the front structure. Glue as you go.

2. Cut 3 quarter-sized circles out of the red paper. Use hot glue to glue these circles to the top of 3 of the 4 structures.

3. Take the 3 unfolded yellow pieces and roll them up the short way. These will be used to connect the 4 parts of the Caterpillar. Apply some glue to 1 end of the yellow "stick" and insert it into a hole between 2 folded pieces in the yellow row. Add glue to the opposite end of the yellow stick and insert it into another caterpillar structure, keeping the stick level.

4. Using the remaining 2 rolled-up yellow sticks, connect the additional remaining structures. By adjusting where you place the sticks, you can make your Caterpillar's body zigzagged or straight.

5. Trace and cut out the eyes, nose, and mouth. Use hot glue to attach the facial features. See the diagram for placement.

6. Finally, cut out and use all-purpose glue to attach the antennae.

7. Feel free to add even more body sections if you like!

LADYBUG

Ladybug

Many people think ladybugs are a sign of good luck. Instead of waiting for a real one to show up on your windowsill, make one! Actually, make two—one to keep and one to give as a gift. The eyes are made out of white and black paper, but you can substitute googly eyes if you have some. Same with the antennae—I used pipe cleaners, but if you don't have any on hand, just use strips of black paper. The finished product is approximately 4" high and 4" wide.

Materials

* 70 Size A Black Folded Pieces (24 lb. paper)
* 159 Size A Red Folded Pieces (24 lb. paper)
* 46 Size A Tan Folded Pieces (20 lb. paper)
* 25 Size A White Folded Pieces (24 lb. paper)—used for foundation row; any color can be substituted
* All-Purpose Glue
* Scissors
* Black Pipe Cleaner (for antennae)
* Black and White Paper (65 lb. cardstock)—for eyes
* Hot Glue Gun
* Black Paper (65 lb. cardstock)—for mouth

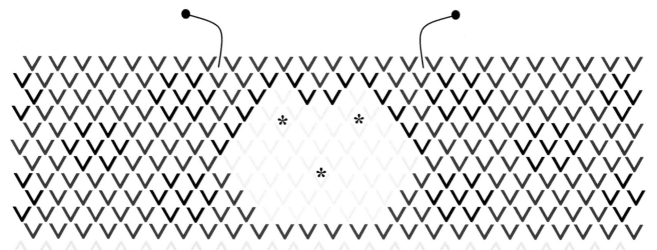

Key

∧ Smooth side facing out (these pieces will not be visible when the structure is complete since they serve as a foundation for the structure to be built on)

V Rough side facing out

* Placement of eyes and mouth

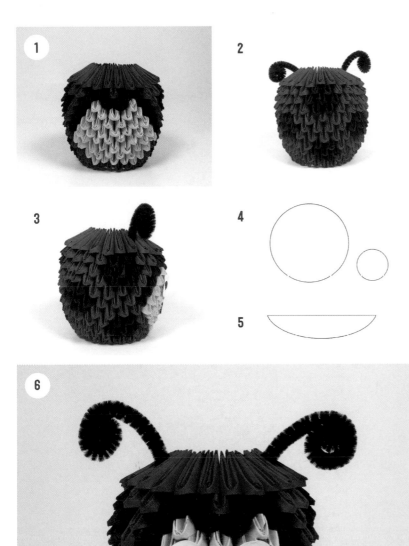

1. Start this Ladybug with the basic 3D origami base. (See the instructions for "How to Construct a Base" in Chapter 1.) Use 25 pieces of white paper where Chapter 1 shows orange pieces, as well as 25 pieces for row 1 (shown in blue in Chapter 1). Follow the color pattern in the diagram and construct all the way to the top. Each piece being added will connect 2 different pieces from the previous row. There will be 25 pieces in each row and a total of 11 rows. Glue as you go.

2. The spots of this Ladybug are symmetrical, just like the real thing. Follow the color pattern in the diagram.

3. Cut the pipe cleaner into 2 (3") pieces. Curl the tips of the pipe cleaners to make a spiral. Insert them into your structure and secure with all-purpose glue. (Placement is shown on the diagram.)

4. Cut the black and white paper into circles for the eyes (big circles with the white, small circles with the black). Glue to the structure using hot glue.

5. Cut a semicircle out of the black paper for the mouth. Glue it to the structure using hot glue.

6. I thought she looked especially friendly with her mouth slightly askew, but place it however you like it.

SUNFLOWER

Sunflower

Real flowers are wonderful, but require a lot of care and can make some people sneeze! This 8" 3D origami flower is a beautiful alternative—it will look great for a long time and is just as thoughtful. Make several in varying colors to give a full bouquet! The smaller pieces in the materials list will be used for the stem and the bigger pieces will be used for the flower itself. Remember to glue as you construct to ensure your work of art remains intact.

Materials

* 54 Size A Yellow Folded Pieces (24 lb. paper)
* 36 Size A Brown Folded Pieces (24 lb. paper)
* All-Purpose Glue
* 76 Size B Green Folded Pieces (24 lb. paper)
* Hot Glue Gun
* 1 Large Black Pompom

Key
V Rough side facing upward
(structure lies horizontally)
Λ Smooth side facing upward
(structure lies horizontally)
* Where petals are inserted

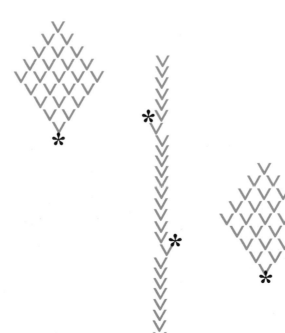

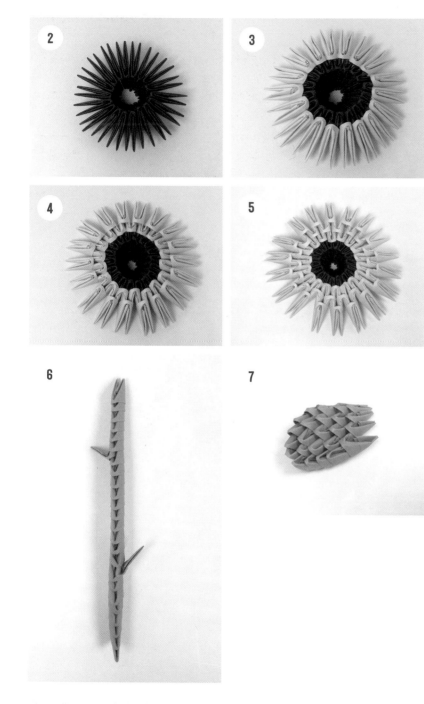

1. Most 3D origami structures are constructed from the bottom up. This design follows the same 3D origami base, but is constructed from the inside out. (See the instructions for "How to Construct a Base" in Chapter 1.) You will not carry out step 7, flattening of the base. There are 18 pieces in each row. Construct outward from the middle and follow the diagram. Glue as you go.

2. Use 18 brown pieces where Chapter 1 shows orange pieces, followed by another row of 18 brown pieces for row 1 (shown in blue in Chapter 1).

3. Next, build a row of yellow pieces around row 1. Each piece you add should pocket the points of 2 different pieces from the previous row.

4. Add another row of yellow pieces.

5. Add a final row of yellow pieces to complete the petals of the flower.

6. Construct the Sunflower stem following the diagram. When you reach the 8th and 18th piece from the bottom, the next piece will be inserted only on the outer point. The piece will stick out and serve as a place of attachment for the leaf.

7. Follow the diagram for the leaf and construct from the bottom to the top. Notice how the pieces increase for a few rows. On the increasing rows, the outer pieces will have an extra pocket that is not inserted into a point. (It does not matter which pocket is left empty.) On row 5, where the first decrease takes place, the outer pieces will pocket 3 points instead of 2. This gives the leaf a smoother edge.

8. Insert the 2 leaves into the points sticking out from the stem. Glue in place.

9. Use hot glue to attach the stem to the flower. You may glue in any space between the petals—just nudge them aside a bit and insert the stem.

10. Glue the black pompom into the center of the flower. Done—with all of the beauty of a real flower but none of the maintenance!

BUMBLEBEE

Bumblebee

This cheerful little 3" Bumble-bee will buzz its way right into your heart! The simple design only uses 180 pieces, so it's a good choice for beginners. If you're going to make this with kids, consider cutting and folding the necessary pieces ahead of time so you can jump right into assembly.

Materials

* 100 Size A Yellow Folded Pieces (24 lb. paper)
* 80 Size A Black Folded Pieces (24 lb. paper)
* All-Purpose Glue
* Scissors
* Black Pipe Cleaner (for antennae)
* Hot Glue Gun
* Black and White Paper (65 lb. cardstock)—for eyes
* Black Paper (65 lb. cardstock)—for mouth
* White Paper (65 lb. cardstock)—for wings

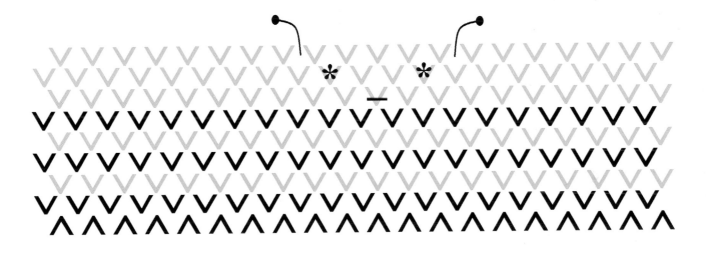

Key
∧ Smooth side facing out (these pieces will not be visible when the structure is complete since they serve as a foundation for the structure to be built on)
∨ Rough side facing out
Black Curved Lines Placement of antennae
∗ Placement of eyes
— Placement of mouth

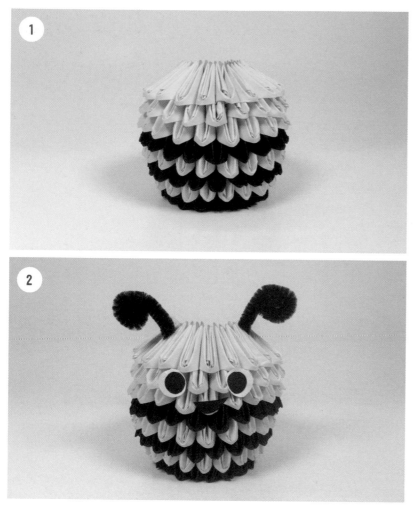

1. Start this Bumblebee with the basic 3D origami base. (See the instructions for "How to Construct a Base" in Chapter 1.) Use 20 pieces where Chapter 1 shows orange, as well as 20 pieces for row 1 (shown in blue in Chapter 1). Follow the diagram for the color pattern. Each folded piece added to a row will attach to 2 different pieces from the previous row. Glue as you go.

2. Cut the pipe cleaner into 2 (3") pieces. Curl the tips of the pipe cleaners to make a spiral. Insert into your structure and secure with hot glue. Placement is shown on the diagram.

3. Cut the black and white paper into circles for the eyes (the black circles will be smaller so they can be glued within the white circles). Hot glue the eyes to the structure where shown.

4. Cut the black paper into a semicircle for the mouth. Attach to the structure with hot glue.

3

4

5

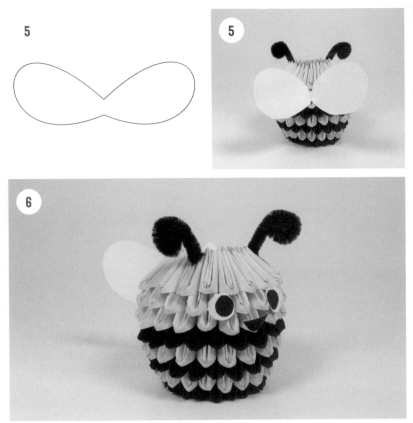

5. Fold the white paper in half and cut out an oval shape, leaving a portion of the folded part uncut. Open it up and you have wings. Use hot glue to attach to the back of the Bumblebee.

6. She's ready to fly!

SEA TURTLE

Sea Turtle

A sea turtle's unique paddle-like flippers are captured perfectly in this design. Remember, 3D origami is versatile when it comes to size. If you want a bigger turtle (the directions here will give you a 3"-long one), increase the size of your 3D origami folded pieces. To do this you could use 2.5" × 3" paper pieces, which is slightly bigger than Size A paper. Or perhaps change the pieces to Size B folded pieces to make a baby sea turtle.

Materials

* 48 Size A Light Green Folded Pieces (24 lb. paper)
* 40 Size A Green Folded Pieces (24 lb. paper)
* All-Purpose Glue
* Scissors
* Light Blue Paper (65 lb. cardstock)—for eyes
* Black Marker
* Hot Glue Gun

Key
V Rough side facing upward (structure lies horizontally)
Λ Smooth side facing upward (structure lies horizontally)
✱ Placement of limbs

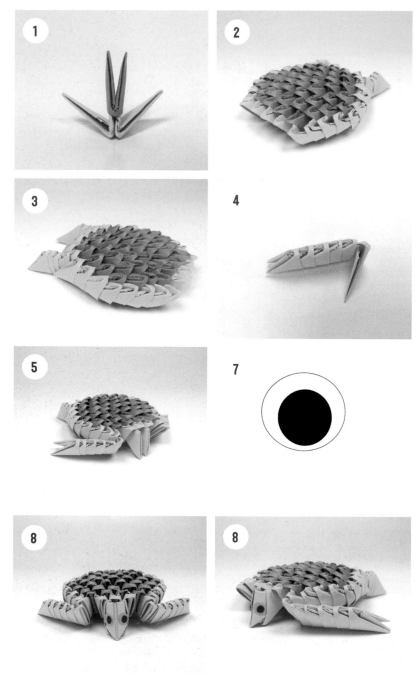

1. The body of the Sea Turtle will be constructed from the head down (bottom to top on diagram). Start by holding 2 light green folded pieces next to each other with the rough side facing toward you. Take the darker green folded piece (facing same direction) and insert it into the light green points so that it connects the 2 light green pieces.

2. Continue constructing so that you have 5 light green pieces across, with 4 darker green pieces constructed above and connecting them. On row 2, you will also insert a light green piece on each outer corner. Since you are "increasing" in this row, there will be an extra unused pocket. It does not matter which pocket you use. Continue to follow the diagram and don't forget to glue as you construct.

3. On row 6, the pieces will start decreasing. In order to keep the shape of the Sea Turtle smooth on the side, the outer pieces will "pocket" 3 points.

4. Follow the diagram and construct and glue the Sea Turtle's flippers. Don't forget to glue.

5. Insert the flippers into the body of the Sea Turtle. Take 2 light green folded pieces and insert them, smooth side facing up, into the front of the body. See the diagram for placement. This will be the head of the turtle.

6. With your last light green folded piece, insert it smooth side up into the pieces from the last step. Be sure to insert the points into the outer pockets to widen the head of the turtle.

7. Cut out eyes using the blue paper and color an inner black circle on them with black marker. Glue your eyes on the sides of this final piece using all-purpose glue.

8. Your Sea Turtle is complete!

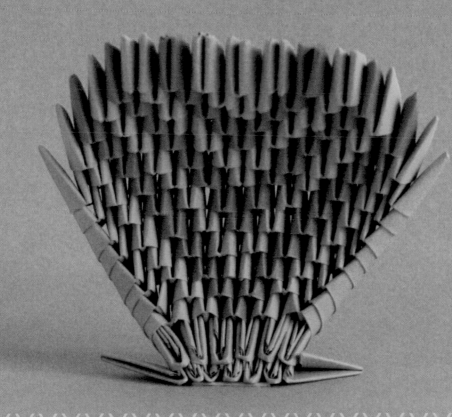

SEASHELL

Seashell

This beautiful 4" Seashell captures both textures of 3D origami—one on each side of the shell. This one has tons of color potential, so personalize yours however you like. This is a simple design that's easy to customize for room decor or a party centerpiece.

Materials

✳ 83 Size A Turquoise Folded Pieces (24 lb. paper)

✳ 43 Size A Purple Folded Pieces (24 lb. paper)

✳ All-Purpose Glue

Key
∧ Smooth side facing out (these pieces will not be visible when the structure is complete since they serve as a foundation for the structure to be built on)
∨ Rough side facing out

1. This Seashell is constructed from the bottom up. However, the bottom-most row in the diagram will be added at the very end. Start by taking 2 turquoise folded pieces and hold them next to each other with their points up and smooth side facing you. Face the rough side of a purple piece toward you and wedge open the pockets on the bottom. Insert it into the middle points of the first 2 pieces. This should connect the pieces. Since the amount of pieces decreases from row 1 to row 2, the outer pieces should pocket 3 points to avoid flaps sticking out. Image A shows the front view and Image B shows the back.

2. Follow the diagram and continue building upward. The structure will get wider for 8 consecutive rows. For these 8 rows, there will always be an extra pocket for the outer pieces. For the last 5 constructing rows, there will be a decrease in pieces; therefore there will be an extra point on both sides of these rows. Don't forget to glue as you construct!

3. Now you will build the bottom-most row that will give your structure more support and allow it to stand vertically. Insert the points of turquoise folded pieces into the pockets at the bottom of the seashell. Follow the diagram for placement. The smooth side should be facing you. Each piece added should connect to the pockets of 2 different pieces.

4. For the outer pieces in this bottom-most row, place the inner points in the pockets and allow the extra point to hang out. This gives the Seashell the final look and support it needs.

5. Carefully adjust your Seashell as needed to make it balance. You can do this by gently bending the structure to form an elegant curve. See photos for front and back views.

CLOWN FISH

Clown Fish

This 6" long structure is built upward, but when it's complete, it lies sideways for display. This makes it different from the other 3D origami designs. Make a whole school of these to "swim" together! If the traditional clown fish colors aren't your favorite, swap with your choice to make a different type of fish.

Materials

* 155 Size A Orange Folded Pieces (24 lb. paper)
* 74 Size A Black Folded Pieces (24 lb. paper)
* 37 Size A White Folded Pieces (24 lb. paper)
* All-Purpose Glue
* Hot Glue Gun
* Scissors
* White Paper (65 lb. cardstock)—for eyes
* Black Marker

Key
V Rough side facing out
* Placement of eyes
Arrow Where tail is glued
Black Dot Part of the tail that's glued to the body

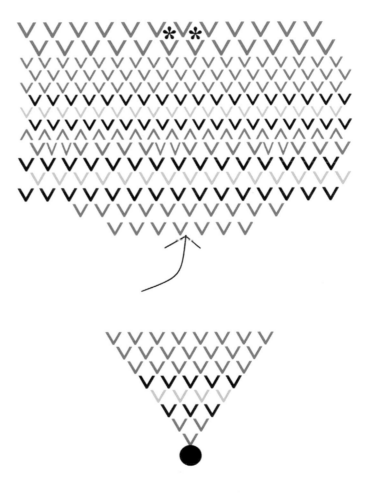

1. This clownfish does not use the typical 3D origami base. Instead, start constructing with the first black row from the bottom in the top part of the diagram (the body). There are 15 pieces in this row. We will add the 2 bottom orange rows later.

2. Start by taking 2 black folded pieces. Place them next to each other with their points up and rough side facing toward you. Take a white folded piece (color of next row, depicted in diagram) and insert the points of the black pieces into the pockets of the white piece. These pieces should all be facing the same direction. The white piece should now connect both black pieces. Continue building your pieces as it shows in the diagram, until you have 15 black pieces across. The ends of the 15-piece black row will be joined by a white piece. The following row of white pieces should also have 15 pieces. You should have made a circle by this point. Glue as you go.

3. Construct another row of 15 black pieces, making sure that every piece you add connects to the points of 2 different pieces from the previous row. The next row of orange folded pieces (as seen in the diagram) has an increase of 3 pieces, for a total of 18 pieces across. This is to widen the belly of the Clownfish. To increase in this row, you will have 4 normally constructed pieces followed by 2 pieces that will share the space of 2 points. This means that 1 pocket from each of these 2 pieces will not be filled. (For example, see the orange pocket not filled 6 rows from the bottom, in the middle.) Repeat this pattern for this entire row. Construct the next row like normal. It will now have 18 pieces across due to the increase from the previous row.

4. Continue constructing up the diagram. Don't forget to glue! When you get to the second orange row from the top, it's time to decrease. Instead of 18 pieces, this row will have 12 pieces. For every piece inserted, you will fit 3 points into the pockets. It doesn't matter which pocket gets 1 or 2 points. Repeat this all around.

5. Now to finish the back end of the Clownfish. There will be a decrease in pieces. Insert the points of an orange folded piece (facing the same direction as the black row) into the pockets of the black row's pieces, leaving an empty pocket in between.

6. Continue this pattern all the way around. There are 10 orange pieces in this row.

7. This next row will be constructed into the pockets of the pieces in the previous step. There is another decrease in pieces, this time down to 7 pieces. You will be following the same pattern as the previous step and inserting the points into every other pocket all the way around. The pieces aren't quite as even, so you will be left with 2 pockets, in which your last piece will fit nicely.

8. Follow the diagram to construct the tail for the Clownfish.

9. Glue the tail to the Clownfish using a hot glue gun.

10. Cut out the eyes using the white paper. Color in the inner centers using black marker. Use hot glue to attach the eyes to the Clownfish.

11. Finished!

OCTOPUS

Octopus

This Octopus is one of my favorites and so much fun to make. I chose complementary pastel colors for mine, but customize yours to your liking. One of the cool things about this design is you can leave out the tentacles and facial features, and you have yourself a nice 3" tall 3D origami Easter Egg!

Materials

* 99 Size A Pastel Blue Folded Pieces (24 lb. paper)
* 86 Size A Pastel Yellow Folded Pieces (24 lb. paper)
* 107 Size A Pastel Purple Folded Pieces (24 lb. paper)
* 21 Size A White Folded Pieces (24 lb. paper)

* All-Purpose Glue
* Scissors
* Purple Paper (65 lb. cardstock)— for eyes and mouth
* Black Marker
* Hot Glue Gun

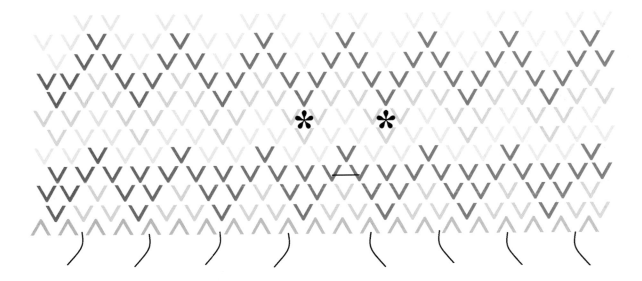

Key

∧ Smooth side facing out (these pieces will not be visible when the structure is complete since they serve as a foundation for the structure to be built on)

∨ Rough side facing out

✳ Placement of eyes

— Placement of mouth

Black Lines Where tentacles will be inserted

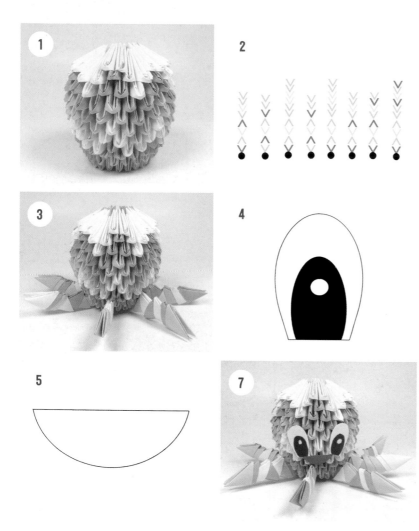

1. Start with "How to Construct a Base" (see Chapter 1) and make a 21-piece foundation. I used white pieces for the base since it's not visible from the outside of the structure. Follow the pattern on the diagram all the way to the top. Glue as you go. If you stop here, you have an Easter egg shape. (It doesn't stand up the other way, but it would look lovely in a bowl with others!)

2. Use the diagram to construct the tentacles. The pattern I made is just random, so feel free to make up your own.

3. Insert 8 of the tentacles into the lower gaps of the structure. Use your eye to space them out so it looks even, or follow the diagram if you'd like to be exact. The black lines represent where tentacles can be inserted.

4. Cut out an eye shape from the purple paper. Black in part of the eye with a marker, leaving a small white circle to give the eye some depth and personality.

5. Now cut out the mouth shape.

6. Use hot glue to attach the eyes and mouth to the body of the Octopus. Your origami Octopus will swim into someone's heart!

CRAB

Crab

This snappy red 2" Crab uses only 47 pieces, so it's great for a beginner's project. The shape of the folded 3D origami pieces looks just like a crab's claws. I used 24-pound red paper for this design, but you could use 20-pound paper instead in this case because smaller-sized projects (especially those that lie flat) are less likely to show the less sturdy/crispy aspect with thinner paper, versus large projects that have multiple rows.

Materials

* 48 Size A Red Folded Pieces (24 lb. paper)
* All-Purpose Glue
* Scissors
* White Paper (65 lb. cardstock)—for eyes
* Black Marker
* Hot Glue Gun

Key
V Rough side facing upward
(structure lies horizontally)
✱ Placement of eyes

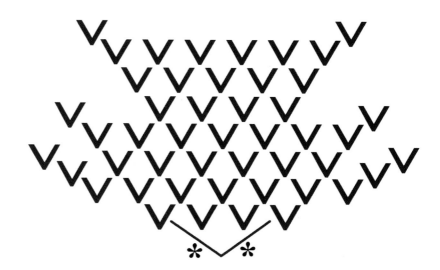

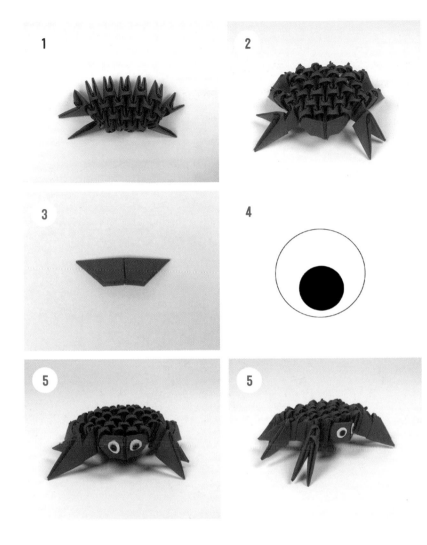

1. This Crab structure lies horizontally, so remember to glue as you construct or your pieces will fall apart. This particular design is simple because all the pieces face the same direction. There is increasing and decreasing in rows to help extend the claws. Start at the bottom of the diagram (ignore the face for now). Take 2 red folded pieces and face the rough side toward you. Take a third red piece and insert the points of the first 2 red pieces into the pockets of the third piece. You should have all pieces connected. Continue adding to this so that you have 4 pieces across the bottom row, held together by 3 pieces above. Insert the outer pieces of row 2 into the outer points remaining from row 1. This will give you 5 pieces in row 2. The remaining 2 pieces of row 2 will be added after the next row is constructed. Follow the diagram and continue to construct.

2. You'll notice in the diagram that some of the pieces seem to extend out. These will be the Crab's claws and legs. When inserting the extending pieces, make sure to only insert the point into 1 pocket of the building piece. This will allow the 3D origami piece to fan open and appear more like a claw. Continue following the diagram and glue the pieces as you build.

3. For the face of the Crab, you will take a single red folded piece and unfold it so you get a bigger triangle. Cut off the tip with scissors. Insert this piece into the front of the Crab so that it stretches out all across the front. Insert and glue it into the outermost pockets.

4. Add the eyes. Cut 2 circles from white paper and color smaller black circles inside.

5. Use all-purpose glue to attach the eyes to the front of the face. See the diagram for placement.

Chapter 6
FARM ANIMALS

Owl

Sure, owls found in nature aren't bright blue and neon pink, but sometimes it's fun to mix things up. This woodland creature is very popular in kids' gear now, and this design is perfect for fall or Halloween decor, either for everyday use or for a party. The finished 2.5" tall Owl's ears and nose add to her silly temperament.

Materials

* 24 Size A Pink Folded Pieces (24 lb. paper)
* 110 Size A Blue Folded Pieces (24 lb. paper)
* All-Purpose Glue
* Scissors
* White and Black Paper (65 lb. cardstock)—for eyes
* Hot Glue Gun
* 1 (3 × 1.5 cm) Pink Folded Piece (24 lb.)—for nose

Key
∧ Smooth side facing out (these pieces will not be visible when the structure is complete since they serve as a foundation for the structure to be built on)
∨ Rough side facing out
∗ Placement of eyes and nose

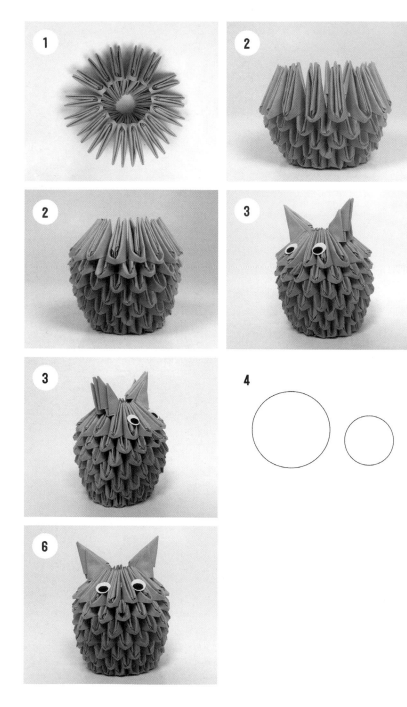

1. Create a basic 3D origami base. (See the instruction for "How to Construct a Base" in Chapter 1.) Use 16 pieces where Chapter 1 shows orange pieces, as well as 16 pieces for row 1 (shown in blue in Chapter 1).

2. The pink pieces will make up the belly. Each piece added to the structure should connect 2 pieces from the previous row. Glue as you go.

3. For the ears, insert the pieces with the smooth side facing out. The ears build on the previous row and connect 2 different pieces, just as you've been doing all along. The diagram shows the placement of the pieces. Don't forget to glue in place!

4. Take your white and black paper for the eyes and cut them into circles (small circles for the black, bigger circles for the white). Glue the black circles within the white circles (feel free to make them cross-eyed, crazy-eyes, or whatever you want!). Use hot glue to attach the eyes (see the diagram for placement).

5. Take your 3 × 1.5 cm pink folded piece and use all-purpose glue to attach it to the structure for the Owl's nose. The diagram shows the placement of the nose.

6. This Owl is ready to guard a barn or provide spooky "whoooo" sounds on Halloween!

COW

Cow

This 6.5" 3D origami Cow is made up of a whopping 667 pieces! Don't let the number intimidate you, though. In fact, I like bigger designs like this because it's possible to close off the bottom and use the structure as a pencil holder. That gives your piece of art a function beyond just being cute. Use the same thickness of paper throughout the whole structure to avoid unevenness. You can find both 24-pound white and black paper online.

Materials

* 513 Size A White Folded Pieces (24 lb. paper)
* 154 Size A Black Folded Pieces (24 lb. paper)
* All-Purpose Glue
* Scissors
* White and Black Paper (65 lb. cardstock)—for eyes and arms
* Pink Paper (65 lb. card-stock)—for nose
* Black Marker
* White and Pink Paper (65 lb. cardstock)—for ears and horns
* Hot Glue Gun

Key

Λ Smooth side facing out (these pieces will not be visible when the structure is complete since they serve as a foundation for the structure to be built on)

V Rough side facing out

* Placement of eyes

Black Lines—Placement of ears and horns, arms, and nose

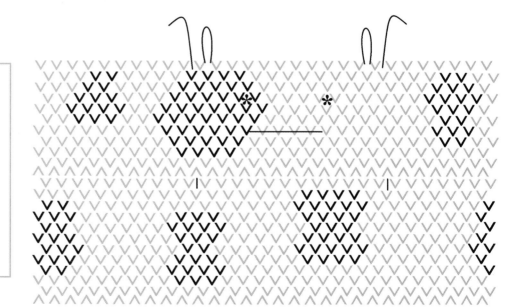

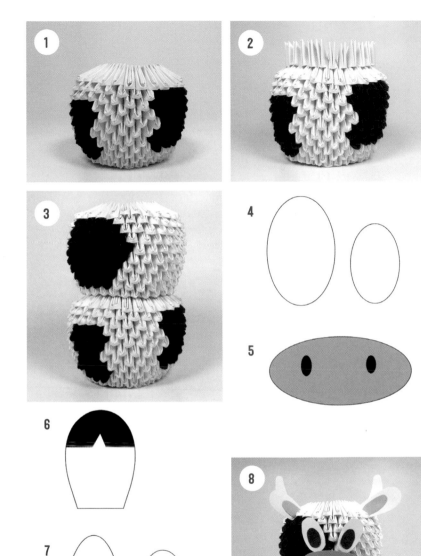

1. Start with "How to Construct a Base" in Chapter 1. There will be 29 pieces in each row of this part of the Cow. As you build upward, the pieces you add should connect 2 points from the previous row.

2. When the pieces switch to the smooth side facing out, you're creating a new foundation in which the head can be built on. Be sure to glue as you construct.

3. Continue following the diagram and constructing the pieces for this Cow until you reach the top. Now you're ready to add facial features.

4. Cut out the Cow's eyes from white and black paper.

5. Create the Cow's pink nose from pink paper and a black marker.

6. Next up: His arms! Use black and white paper.

7. Finally, create his ears with pink and white paper.

8. Use hot glue to attach the Cow's eyes and nose. For the horns, ears, and limbs, using regular glue is fine. See the diagram for placement. Moooo!

BABY CHICK

Baby Chick

This 4" Baby Chick is made up of 280 pieces. At first, I set off to make a chicken, but when I saw the pastel yellow paper, I knew a baby chick would be even cuter. Make yourself a nice little flock of 4–5 of these little guys. Perfect for a springtime display!

Materials

* 280 Size A Pastel Yellow Folded Pieces (24 or 20 lb. paper)
* All-Purpose Glue
* Scissors
* Orange Paper (65 lb. cardstock)—for beak and feet
* Hot Glue Gun
* Pastel Yellow Paper (65 lb. cardstock)—for wings and feathers
* Black Paper (65 lb. cardstock)—for eyes

Key
∧ Smooth side facing out (these pieces will not be visible when the structure is complete since they serve as a foundation for the structure to be built on)
∨ Rough side facing out
* Placement of eyes
Diamond—Placement of beak
Black Lines—Placement of wings
Triangles—Placement of feet

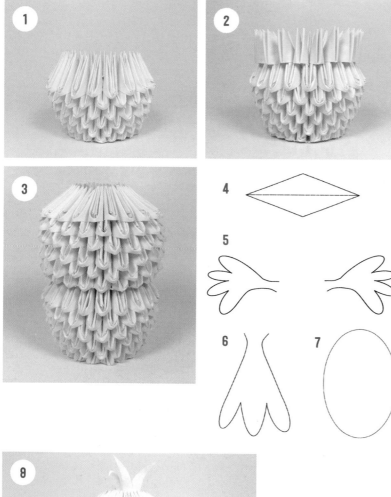

1. Start with "How to Construct a Base" (see Chapter 1). There will be 20 pieces in each row of this Baby Chick. The bottom row in the diagram is the base of the foundation. This will not be visible once the structure is complete, so the color does not matter. For this pattern, I kept it all Pastel Yellow.

2. Row 7 will have the pieces facing smooth side out. By facing the pieces this way, it creates a new foundation in which the head can be built on. Be sure to glue each piece to the structure.

3. Continue constructing upward until you get to the top. That completes the body of the Baby Chick. Now it's time to attach the facial features and limbs.

4. For the beak, cut a diamond shape out of orange paper. Fold it in half to create a beak-like appearance. Hot glue it onto the face.

5. Cut out the wings using yellow paper. Use regular glue to attach the wings to the bird. See the diagram for placement.

6. For the feet, cut orange paper into the shape shown. Hot glue them to the bottom of the structure.

7. Cut out the Chick's eyes using black paper and attach with hot glue.

8. I used remnant scraps of pastel yellow paper for the bird's feathers on its head. Cut them out however you wish, and glue them to the inside to give the chicken some features on its head. Your adorable Baby Chick is complete!

SPIDER

Spider

Spiders don't always have to be creepy! This sweet-look-ing barnyard Spider is 84 pieces of the smaller-sized fold-ing paper and does not follow the typical 3D origami base. The 2" long creature lies flat; therefore instead of building upward, the pieces are built horizontally. It is important to glue as you construct, or you will find your pieces falling apart. Leave him on tables during Halloween season for a friendly touch.

Materials

* 84 Size B Black Folded Pieces (24 lb. paper)
* All-Purpose Glue
* Scissors
* White Paper (65 lb. cardstock)—for eyes
* Black Marker
* Hot Glue Gun
* Yellow Paper (65 lb. cardstock)—for mouth

Key
V Rough side facing upward (structure lies horizontally)
✳ Placement of eyes

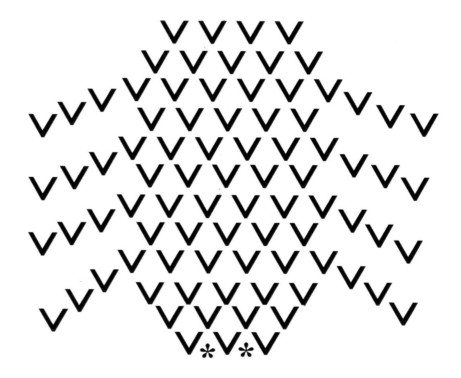

3

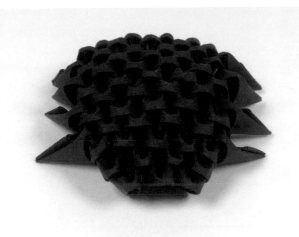

4

1. This Spider lies horizontally when complete. Construction starts at the head of the Spider, which is at the bottom of the diagram. You'll notice the pieces that stick out from the diagram: those are the legs of the Spider. These pieces don't need to be constructed until the main body is completed. Each leg has 3 origami pieces.

2. Start constructing at the head of the Spider. Your first row will have 3 pieces. Start by holding 2 black folded pieces next to each other with their points up and rough side facing you. With a third piece, hold it in the same direction and insert its pockets into the middle points of the first 2 pieces. This should join the first 2 pieces. Glue as you go.

3. You have 3 pieces attached to one another, which makes up part of row 1 and 2 of the diagram. To construct off of this, take another black folded piece and hold it right next to the 2 pieces from row 1. Use another black folded piece and insert it into row 2. This piece's pockets will be inserted into the points of row 1, thus joining the pieces of that row. You should now have 3 pieces in row 1, and 2 pieces in row 2.

4. Continue building and following the diagram. On all rows with 6 pieces across, the outer pieces must be inserted with the point into the inner pocket of that piece. This is so part of the folded piece will hang out from the body and you will have something to construct the legs off of.

5. Construct each leg by taking 3 folded pieces and inserting them directly into one another's pockets (2 points of a piece will be inserted into the 2 pockets of another).

6. The legs will attach to the body at the 8 areas where the flaps are hanging out. Remember to glue!

7. Cut 2 small circles out of white paper and use a black marker to color a smaller circle in the middle. Hot glue the eyes to the structure.

8. Finally, cut the mouth out of yellow paper and hot glue it under the eyes.

9. He's ready to crawl away!

PIG

Pig

Oink! Oink! When displaying this piece, I like to cut out splotches of brown paper and let the Pig sit on top of them, giving the appearance of mud puddles. I used 24-pound paper, but 20-pound would work fine also. This cute little Pig stands about 5" tall.

Materials

* 442 Size A Pink Folded Pieces (24 lb. paper)
* All-Purpose Glue
* Scissors
* Black and White Paper (65 lb. cardstock)—for eyes
* Hot Glue Gun
* Pink Paper (65 lb. cardstock)—for nose, ears, and tail
* Black Marker
* Pink and Black Paper (65 lb. cardstock)—for arms

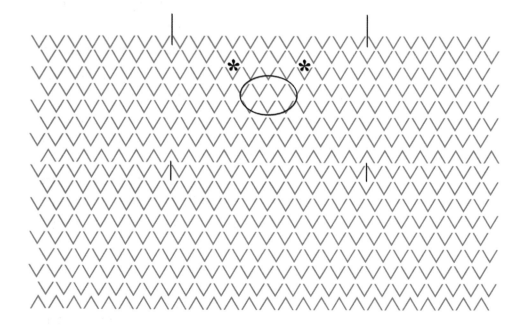

Key

∧ Smooth side facing out (these pieces will not be visible when the structure is complete since they serve as a foundation for the structure to be built on)

∨ Rough side facing out

* Placement of eyes

Black Oval—Placement of nose

| Placement of ears and arms

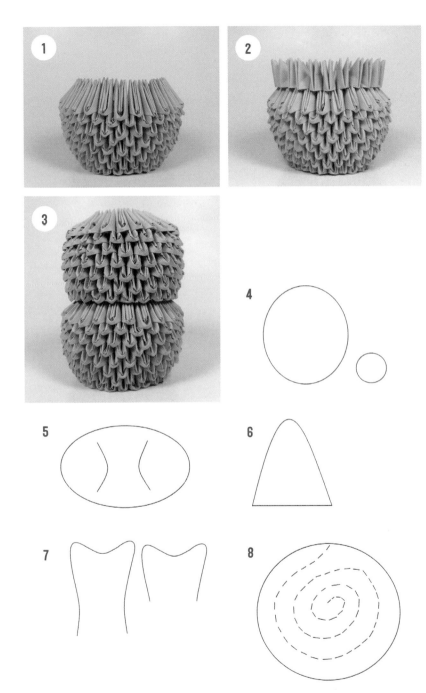

1. Start with "How to Construct a Base" (see Chapter 1). This initial base row of 26 pieces is demonstrated by the orange pieces in Chapter 1 (∧ in the diagram). Row 1 also has 26 pieces and is depicted in blue in Chapter 1. Every row from the bottom up will connect and work off the previous. Remember to glue as your construct.

2. When you get to the row where the pieces face smooth side out, be sure you glue during this step. This row will serve as a foundation for a new base to start. This bump in the structure will be the head of the Pig.

3. Continue constructing all the way to the top.

4. Cut out the Pig's eyes using white and black paper. Attach with hot glue.

5. Cut out the Pig's nose using pink paper. Add nostrils with a black marker. Use hot glue to attach it, overlapping his eyes a bit.

6. Cut out his ears and curve the top of the paper over a bit.

7. For his arms, cut out both shapes. Overlap the black piece onto the pink. Use regular glue to attach.

8. Every pig needs a curly tail! To create one, cut pink paper into a circle. Starting from the outside, cut into the paper with a spiral movement until you get to the middle.

9. Take the end from the middle and insert it into the back of the Pig. Secure with glue.

10. You're finished!

About the Author

Stephanie Martyn was born and raised in Wichita, Kansas. She graduated from WSU with a bachelor of science in medical technology and works as a medical laboratory scientist. With a passion for music, arts, and anything cute and fancy, she's made time to keep 3D origami a favorite hobby since the age of fifteen. Due to the limitations of store-bought 3D origami kits, Stephanie started buying and cutting her own paper to expand her imagination. Ever since then, she's been fulfilling fun ideas and requests for 3D origami. She enjoys taking up new hobbies with her husband and spending quality time with her children. Find Stinkin' Kute Origami on Facebook (*www.facebook.com/stinkinkuteorigami*), YouTube, and Pinterest for Stephanie's latest ideas!